LEADERSHIP STRATEGIES:
The Power of Character

POINTMAN LEADERSHIP INSTITUTE
Ethics training that works

Pointman Leadership Institute has been approved as an Authorized Provider by the
International Association for Continuing Education and Training (IACET),
1760 Old Meadow Road, Suite 500, McLean, VA 22102; (703) 506-3275.

Welcome

We at Pointman Leadership Institute are grateful that you have chosen to attend our foundational seminar, focusing on Leadership Strategies. This strategic material is based on time-tested principles proven to empower leaders with wisdom, conviction and character.

The issue of character, the internal quality of a person, is being recognized worldwide as the pivotal factor in inspiring, trustworthy leadership. We trust you will be motivated and encouraged as you encounter the Eight Character Traits – the main focus of this foundational seminar.

It is our desire that you will become a person of exemplary character, guiding and developing those who follow and depend on you.

Robert L. Vernon
Assistant Chief (ret.) LAPD
Founder, Pointman Leadership Institute

*I hope I shall always possess the firmness and virtue enough
to maintain what I consider the most enviable of all titles, the
character of an honest man.*

George Washington
First President, United States of America

LEADERSHIP STRATEGIES

Learning Outcomes

The student will learn to recognize, describe, explain, and begin to apply the following:

1. The 10 most commonly accepted/desired behaviors of good leaders.

2. The "disconnect" between those behaviors and actual observed performance.

3. 5 key leadership concepts.

4. 10 differences between leadership & management.

5. How inspirational, trustworthy leadership reduces both time and burden for an organization undergoing change.

6. Scholarly conclusions on leadership, vision and character.

7. The foundational role of character in leadership.

8. The 8 essential character traits (and their working definitions) of inspirational, trustworthy leaders.

9. The definition of a "principle."

10. 10 Ancient Principles that have impacted societies for thousands of years.

11. The role principle plays in establishing character.

12. The application of PLI principle and character based leadership in society and organizational development.

The Point Man

In the military, the Pointman is the person chosen to scout the path ahead. Pointmen are the ones who first spot the enemy and any obstacles. They are the valiant, the ones who alert the group to danger and possible ambush. They become the first targets and usually take the first "hits" to protect others who are following. A Pointman gives direction. Pointmen are those responsible for selecting the right path for others to follow.

Table of Contents

Powerful Leadership and Character

Leadership Defined

- Makes goals clearly understood and articulated.

- Shows the way from the _____ .

- Convinces people to follow by_____ .

- _____ excellence in others.

- _____ achievement at maximum potential.

> "To Follow as an act of free choice"

An effective leader is:

- _____(beyond motivational)
- _____(an example to others)

© Pointman Leadership Institute, 2011

Principle Defined

Principles are the "Bedrock" on which effective leadership is built.

- A principle: _____ truth or _____ force.

- A rule of conduct, especially right conduct.

- Reliable, broad statement of _____ that never changes.

Visible Behaviors of a Leader

YOU WRITE: What visible behaviors do good leaders exhibit?

1._____

2._____

3._____

4._____

5._____

6._____

STOP HERE

Powerful Leadership and Character

There is universal, cross cultural agreement.

Visible Behaviors of a Good Leader

- Decisive
- Keeps Commitments
- Good Judgment
- Gives Recognition
- Equips & Supports Followers

- Good Listener
- Consistent
- Fair
- Removes Work Barriers
- Emphasizes Principles Not Just Rules

The Difference Between Leaders and Managers

Leaders

1. Innovates
2. Develops
3. Focus on People and Abilities
4. _____
5. _____
6. _____
7. _____

Managers

1. Administers
2. Maintains
3. Focus on Systems and Structures
4. _____
5. _____
6. _____
7. _____

Leadership at Every Level

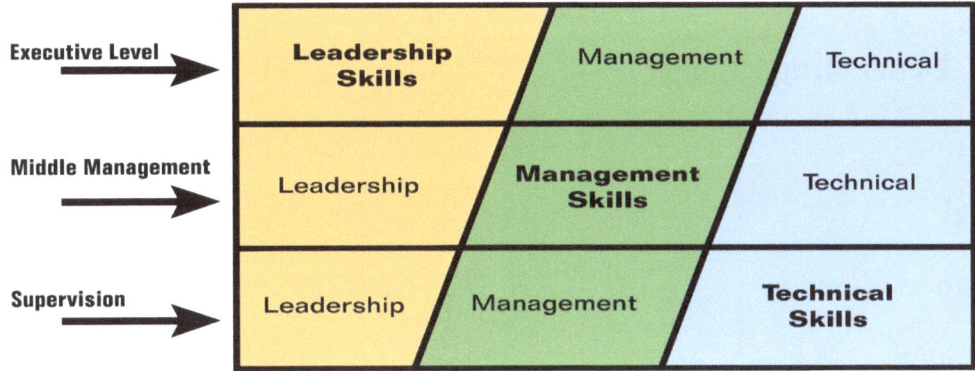

Leaders and Change

YOU WRITE: What forces demand change, what forces resist change?

Demands Change	Resists Change
1. _____	_____
2. _____	_____
3. _____	_____
4. _____	_____
5. _____	_____

Powerful Leadership and Character

A. Forces Affecting Change

Demanding Change	Resisting Change
1. Economics	1. Fear of Unknown
2. Political	2. Fear of Failure
3. International Trends	3. Tradition
4. Technology	4. Vested interests
5. Competition	5. Effort or Work
6. Social	6. Lack of Skills
7. Environmental	7. No Perceived Need
8. Public Expectations	8. Negative Results
9. Legal	9. Habit
10. Current Way is Ineffective	10. Lack of Respect for Leader

B. Change Today Is:

- Significant
  - Rapid
    - Everywhere
      - Inevitable

Navigation requires...
Inspirational, Trustworthy Leaders.

C. Changing Behavior and Attitudes

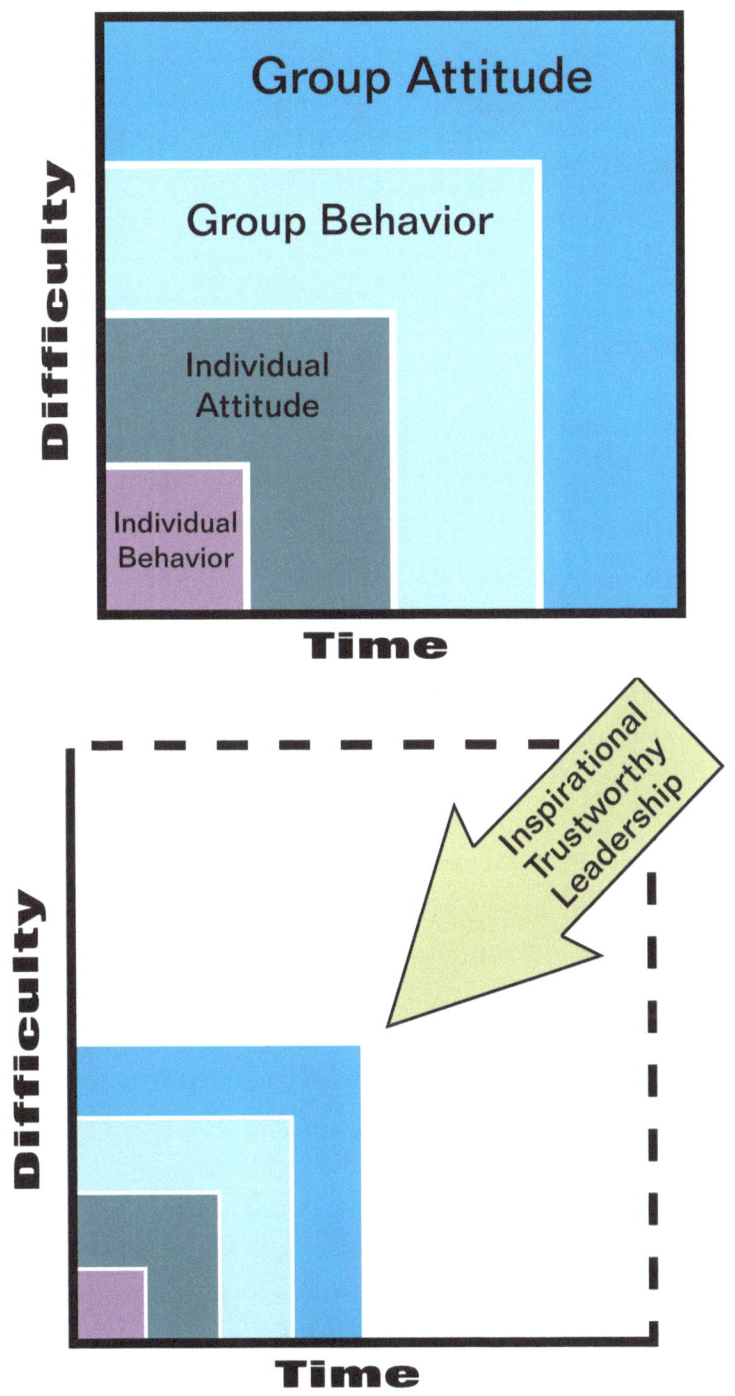

What the Scholars Say

A. **Bennis on Vision**
Develop Vision
    Hard Work
    Involve Others
_____effectively
    Use repetitive methods
    Test for understanding
Retain _____
    Use creative methods

Vision

A mental model of a future state.
- Worthy challenge
- Appropriate for organizational, values and times
- Set a standard of excellence
- Clarify direction
- Inspire enthusiasm and commitment
- Easily understood
- Reflect the uniqueness of the organization

Example

"I will build a motor car for the great multitude. It will be so low in price that no man making a good salary will be unable to own one and enjoy with his family the blessings of hours of pleasure in God's great open spaces...when I am through, everybody will be able to afford one, and everybody will have one. The horse will have disappeared from our highways, the automobile will be taken for granted."

- Henry Ford

Develop Vision   **Communicate**   **Retain the Focus**

B. **Larned on Leadership: Learned, Luck or Lived?**
- Great _____
- Great opportunities
- Great _____

C. **McConnell - Government and Non-profit Leadership**
- Sense of public opinion
- Understanding sources of _____
- Administrative skills
- Negotiating skills
- _____

D. **Phillips - Lincoln on Leadership**
- _____
- Communication
- Tenacity
- _____

Character is Key

Bennis - Inspiring Vision

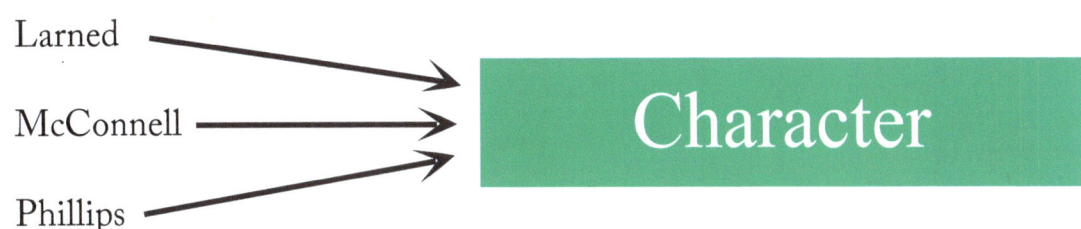

Leadership = Vision and Character

Definition of Character

The result of a consistent, disciplined application —   **Practice / Habits**

of principles —   **Basic Truths**

one has chosen to pursue —   **Values**

Consistent Behavior Demands...

Foundational Character Traits

Integrity Courage Discipline Loyalty
Diligence Humility Optimism Conviction

INTEGRITY
vs. Deception
Actions match stated beliefs

- Oneness vs. _____
- Truthful
- _____
- Believable

Integrity is not something you can turn on and off like a lightbulb!

30 day action plan to sharpen your **Integrity**

At Work: _____

_____

_____

_____

At Home: _____

_____

_____

_____

COURAGE
vs. Cowardice
Overcoming fear, willing to risk

Two major fears that all leaders face.

1. The fear of _____
2. The fear of _____

Courage cannot exist outside the presence of fear.

*   Principle over _____
*   Doing what is _____
*   Seizing the _____

> *"Right is right, even if everyone is against it; and wrong is wrong,*
> *even if everyone is for it."* — **William Penn**

30 day action plan to sharpen your **Courage**

At Work: _____

_____

_____

_____

_____

At Home: _____

_____

_____

_____

DISCIPLINE
vs. Disorder
Maintaining self control

- Remaining calm and composed in _____
- _____and reasonable
- _____

> *"No one wants to give _____ of their life to someone who can't _____ his own"*

30 day action plan to sharpen your **Discipline**

At Work: _____

_____

_____

_____

At Home: _____

_____

_____

_____

Powerful Leadership and Character

LOYALTY
vs. Unfaithfulness
Submission to legitimate authority

- Honor the chain of command
- Being under authority, _____ you authority
- Allegiance/devotion but not _____
- Exceptions: illegal, immoral, unethical

> ## "I lead . . . therefore I follow."

30 day action plan to sharpen your **Loyalty**

At Work: _____

_____

_____

_____

At Home: _____

_____

_____

_____

DILIGENCE
vs. Laziness
Hard work, persistence

- Pursue _____beyond success
- _____orientation
- Commitment

> "*Run the race with* _____
> *and* _____ *of purpose*

30 day action plan to sharpen your **Diligence**

At Work: _____

_____

_____

_____

_____

At Home: _____

_____

_____

_____

Powerful Leadership and Character

HUMILITY
vs. Arrogance
Concern for the interests of others

- Demonstrated by good _____
- Admits when _____
- Results in more ideas and _____
- Demonstrated through the concept of _____ leadership
- Produces compassion and gratitude

30 day action plan to sharpen your **Humility**

At Work: _____

_____

_____

_____

_____

At Home: _____

_____

_____

_____

OPTIMISM
vs. Pessimism
Expecting a good outcome

- Focus on _____ rather than _____
- Realistically address _____
- Expect the _____
- Catch people doing something _____

30 day action plan to sharpen your **Optimism**

At Work: _____

_____

_____

_____

_____

At Home: _____

_____

_____

_____

CONVICTION
vs. Uncertainty
Confidence, certainty and passion

- Founded on knowledge, truth and personal application
- Requires study and _____
- Speaks with _____
- _____creates doubt

Conviction based upon principles creates trust

30 day action plan to sharpen your **Conviction**

At Work: _____

_____

_____

_____

_____

At Home: _____

_____

_____

_____

How Do You Measure Up?

- Integrity
- Courage
- Discipline
- Loyalty

- Diligence
- Humility
- Optimism
- Conviction

Character is built on the bedrock of principle.

Principle

Basic truth, law, doctrine, or inspiring force

Rule of conduct, especially right conduct

Broad statement of Truth

Ten Ancient Principles

- Time tested
- Universal application
- Provides inner compass
- Good results when applied
- Positive impact on society
- Other principles find origin in these ten.

Powerful Leadership and Character

Ten Ancient Principles

1. Submit to Authority

- Understand the importance of the flow of

_____

Action Step: Submit to _____

2. Serve Others First

- Do not serve/pursue gain for yourself exclusively

- No inflated _____

Action Step: Develop a spirit of _____ to others

Ten Ancient Principles

3. Keep Your Commitments

- History: The name of God was used to formalize agreements

- Stabilizes relationships and reduces need for _____

Action Step: Become a person _____

4. Pursue a Balanced Life

- Rest vs. Work

- Especially the balance of the three aspects of human life:

  physical, _____ and Spiritual

Action Step: Evaluate your need to _____ and balance

your life

Ten Ancient Principles

5. Honor Age and Experience

- Show _____ for what you receive from others

- Results in wisdom, tranquility and _____

Action Step: How can you honor those who

have _____

6. Respect All Human Life

- No lesser status based on _____, gender, age

  or _____

Action Step: Become aware of your role in _____who

depend on your leadership and influence

Ten Ancient Principles

7. Protect Your Family

- Importance of _____ institution: _____ fidelity

- _____ to the family is the most

  solemn societal relationship

- Betrayal of family _____ trust in other relationships

Action Step: Make a determined commitment to _____

in all areas of your life

8. Respect the Property of Others

- Goes beyond _____

- Includes _____, vandalism and _____

- _____ social instability and interpersonal conflict

Action Step: Make a personal decision not to _____ from your

work or _____

Ten Ancient Principles

9. Tell the Truth

- To be _____

- Results in _____ _____ respect and compatibility

Action Step: Seek to be straightforward and _____ in

your contacts with others

10. Be Content With What You Have

- Contentment is a _____

- It is possible to have _____ and not be content;

  it is possible to be _____ and be content.

Action Step: Develop a _____ and a positive attitude

The Pointman Commitment

- Integrity

- Courage

- Discipline

- Loyalty

- Diligence

- Humility

- Optimism

- Conviction

Powerful Leadership and Character

It is not the critic who counts; not the man who points out how the strong man stumbles, or where the doer of deeds could have done them better. The credit belongs to the man who is actually in the arena, whose face is marred by dust and sweat and blood; who strives valiantly; who errs, and comes short again and again because there is no effort without error and shortcoming; but who does actually strive to do the deeds; who knows the great enthusiasms, the great devotions; who spends himself in a worthy cause; who at the best knows in the end the triumph of high achievement, and who at the worst, if he fails, at least fails while daring greatly, so that his place shall never be with those cold and timid souls who know neither victory nor defeat.

Theodore Roosevelt
26th President, United States of America

APPENDICES

How does inspirational, trustworthy leadership (vision and character) built on the 10 Ancient Principles benefit an organization and/or society?

Appendix 1 - Organizational Life Cycle

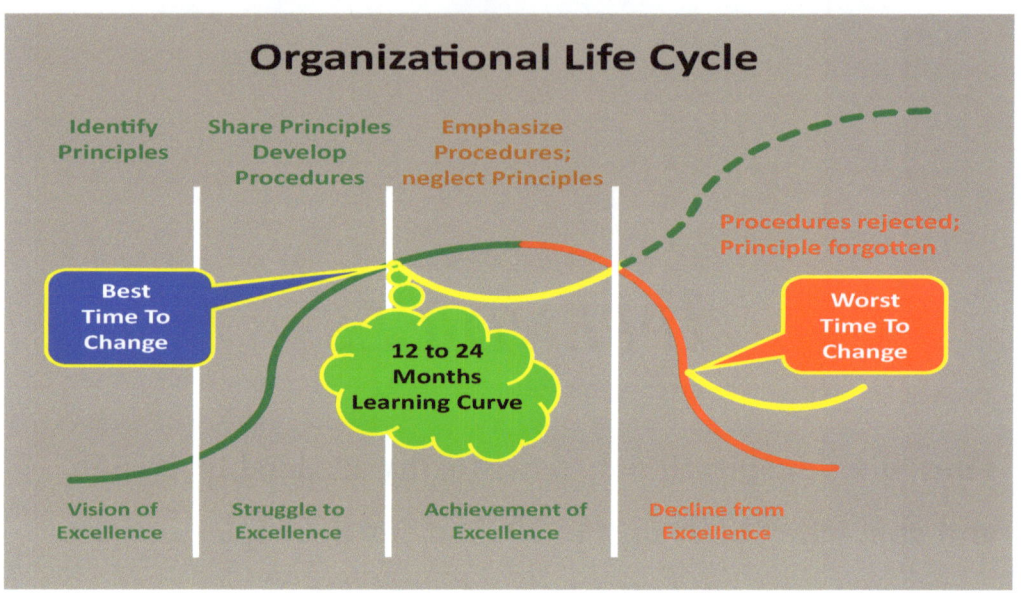

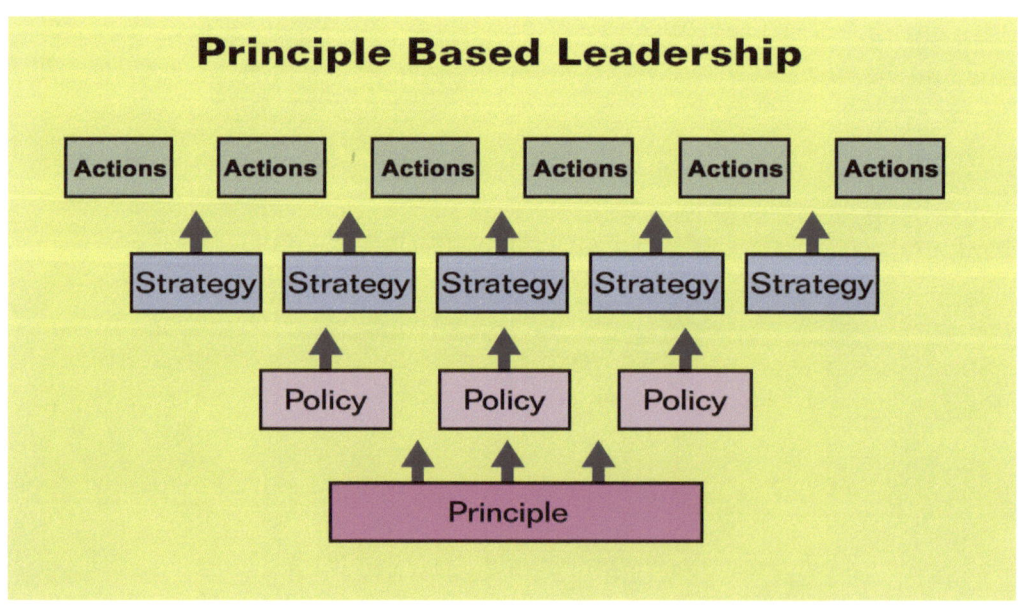

Inspirational, Trustworthy Leadership Develops:

- Conviction to Principles

- Critical mass of commitment to Principles

- Specific objectives and strategies

- Detailed plan with specific tactics

- Subordinates equipped to take action

- Consensus and measurable milestones of achievement

- Institutionalized feedback

- Accountability (positive and negative)

- Consistent reinforcement of Principles

Appendix 2 - Cultural Order

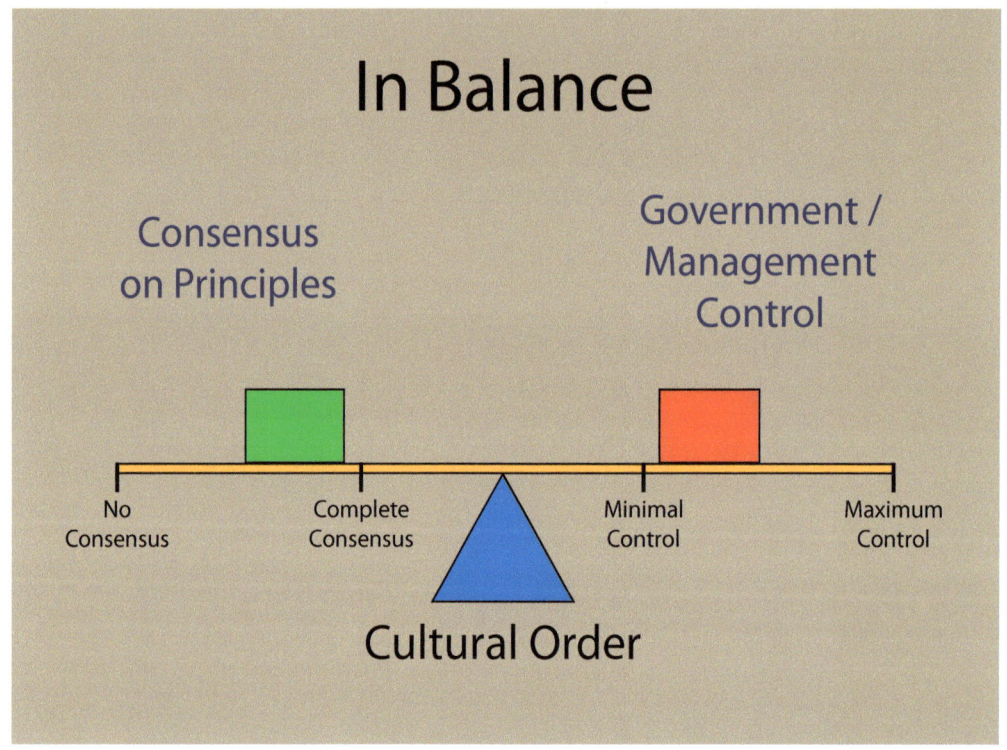

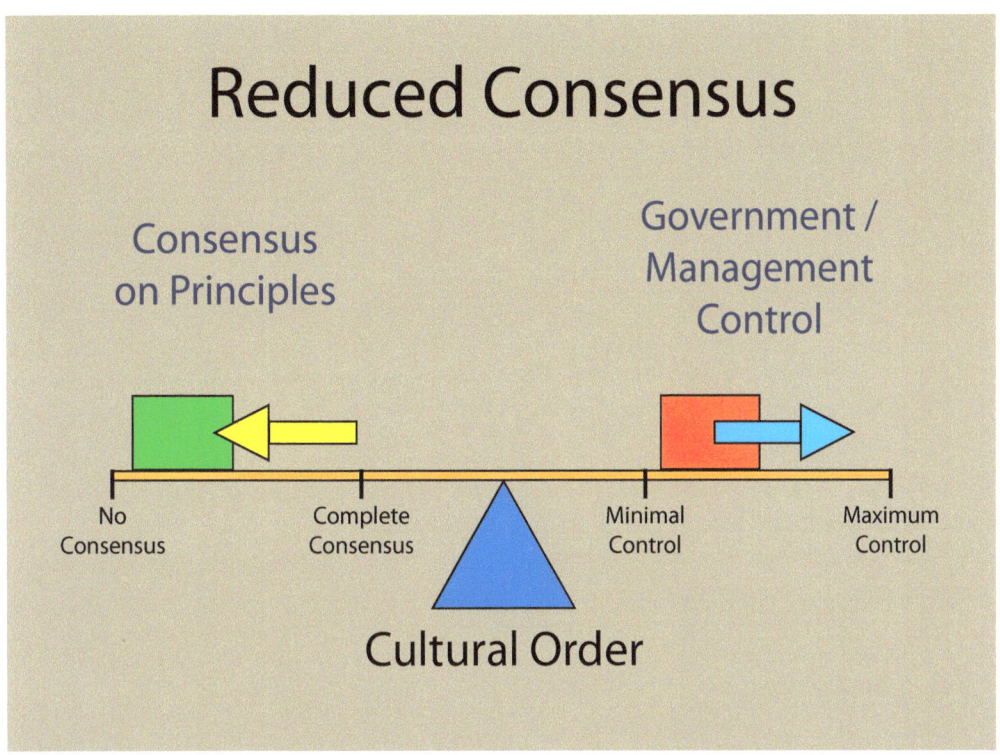

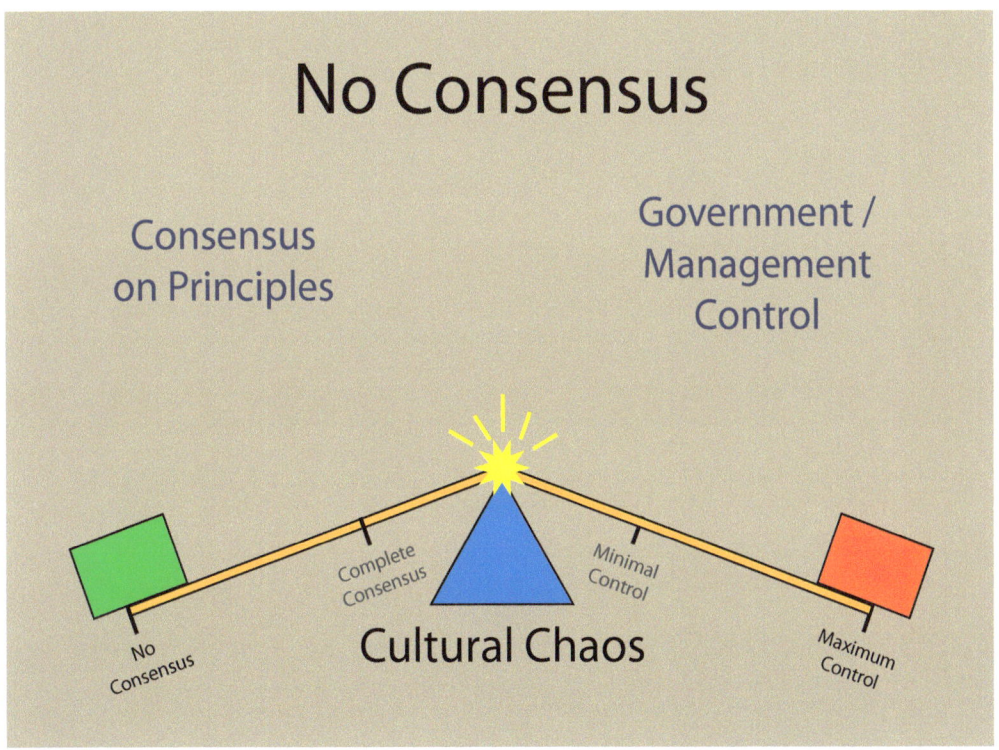

<u>Other PLI Seminars</u>

- Responsible Leadership and Ethics: *Preventing Corruption*

- Advanced Leadership Development

- Custom Seminars

  - Transparent Leadership & Relationships

  - Visionary Leadership & Principles

  - Political Leadership & Society

  - Community-based Policing

  - Strategic Planning

- Consultation and Assessment

Selected PLI Bibliography

- On Becoming a Leader   *Warren Bennis*

- Lincoln on Leadership: Executive Strategies for Tough Times   *Donald T. Phillips*

  - Built to Last: Successful Habits of Visionary Companies*Jim Collins, Jerry I. Porras*

- In Search of Excellence: Lessons from America's Best-Run Companies
  Thomas J. Peters, Robert H. Waterman

- The Speed of Trust: The One Thing That Changes Everything
  Stephen M.R. Covey, Stephen R. Covey, Rebecca R. Merrill

- The Leadership Challenge (4th Edition)   *James M. Kouzes, Barry Z. Posner*

- On Leadership   *John W. Gardner*

- Leadership is an Art   *Max Dupree*

- The Effective Executive   *Peter F. Drucker*

- Integrity   *Stephen L. Carter*

For additional resources go to www.PLIglobal.com/resources.html

Notes:

www.ingramcontent.com/pod-product-compliance
Lightning Source LLC
Chambersburg PA
CBHW040753200526
45159CB00025B/2083